Slithering Snakes

Lynn Huggins-Cooper

A+
Smart Apple Media

First published in 2005 by Franklin Watts
96 Leonard Street, London EC2A 4XD

Franklin Watts Australia
Level 17/207 Kent Street, Sydney NSW 2000

Editor: Jennifer Schofield
Jacket designer and Art director: Peter Scoulding
Designer: Jay Young
Picture researcher: Diana Morris

Acknowledgements:
Kelvin Aitken/Still Pictures: 16. ANTPL/NHPA: 6. Anthony Bannister/Gallo/Corbis: 12.
Anthony Bannister/NHPA: 11, 22, 23, 25. Tobias Bernhard/OSF: 17. Bios/Still Pictures:
18, 19t. John Cancalosi/Still Pictures: front cover r, 5, 20, 21t, 21b. Mary Clay/Ardea: 7.
Compost/Visage/Still Pictures: 28. Tony Crocetta/Still Pictures: 27. James Gerholdt/
Still Pictures: 29. Joachin Gutierrez/OSF: 19b. Daniel Heuchin/NHPA: front cover cl, 15.
Geoff Higgins/OSF: 8. Brian Kenny/OSF: 10. Montford/Still Pictures: 26. OSF: front cover
bl, 24. Photocyclops/Ecoscene: 1, 4, 13. Jeffrey L. Rottman/Corbis: 14. David Williams: 9.

Published in the United States by Smart Apple Media
2140 Howard Drive West, North Mankato, Minnesota 56003

Printed in the United States of America

Library of Congress Cataloging-in-Publication Data

Huggins-Cooper, Lynn.
Slithering snakes / by Lynn Huggins-Cooper.
p. cm. — (Killer nature)
Originally published: London : Franklin Watts, 2005.
ISBN-13 : 978-1-58340-934-3
1. Snakes—Juvenile literature. I. Title.

QL666.O6H855 2006
597.96—dc22   2005051617

9 8 7 6 5 4 3 2 1

Contents

Slithering snakes

Around the world, snakes are kept as pets. And snakes such as this king cobra are admired for their beautiful skin and unusual, hooded heads. But many people shudder at the thought of such a gruesome pet, with its sharp, vampire-like fangs and flicking tongue.

Fact!

Snakes are reptiles, but they are different from other reptiles because they have no ears, eyelids, or limbs.

Killer bites

It is thought that 5 million people are bitten by snakes each year, causing about 125,000 deaths. Although this seems scary, you have a higher risk of being struck by lightning than of being killed by a snake bite.

Friend or foe?

So how can you tell whether a snake is a friend or a foe? Are all snakes dangerous? Is that a twig lying on the ground, or is it a deadly rattlesnake waiting to strike? Read on to find out. It just might save your life one day!

Terrible taipans

Taipans are large, poisonous, and very aggressive. These three things make them one of the most deadly types of snakes in the world.

There are two kinds of taipans: the inland taipan and the coastal taipan. Both kinds are found in northern Australia.

Vital statistics

Taipans are huge snakes. They can measure up to 11 feet (3.4 m) long.

Their fangs are a frightening .4 to .5 inches (11–12 mm) long and are filled with dangerous venom.

Fact!
The venom in a single taipan bite is enough to kill up to 12,000 guinea pigs.

Encounters with people

Taipans are attracted to the places where prey animals such as rats and mice are found. This includes barns, garbage dumps, farms, and houses. Many people live near or at these sites, so this brings these dangerous snakes into contact with humans.

In just a single bite, a taipan can inject enough venom to kill several adults. The good news is that these snakes will not usually bite unless they are cornered or attacked. But if they do attack, they are likely to bite many times.

How they kill

These deadly snakes hunt during the day, killing lizards, birds, and small mammals. Taipans have a sharp sense of smell and very good eyesight.

They strike quickly, injecting enough poison into their prey to kill their victim instantly. The snakes eat their prey as soon as it is killed.

More about taipans

Young taipans

Female taipans lay between 10 and 20 soft-shelled eggs. The eggs hatch in 61 to 84 days. Often, the first set of eggs is followed by a second set between 37 and 69 days later.

Real-life story

In 1995, nurse Ann Wakefield was bitten by a taipan. She did not even see the dangerous snake until after it had attacked her. Luckily, an ambulance rushed Ann to the hospital.

As a nurse, Ann knew exactly what to do while she waited for the ambulance. She tied her shirt tightly around her leg, above the bite, to keep the venom from moving through her body. However, the deadly venom affected her quickly.

Her eyes were blurry, and she could not see clearly. She also had awful stomach cramps and could not breathe properly.

Ann's kidneys did not work for three days, and she was in pain for six weeks after she left the hospital. Parts of her leg are still numb today, but she is incredibly lucky that the doctor treating her had the taipan antidote that saved her life.

Milking a taipan

In the early 1950s, if you were bitten by one of these beasts, you would not survive. However, a snake expert named Eric Worrell managed to "milk" a taipan to make an antidote.

This means that he held the snake's head as it "bit" a container. The venom collected in the container and was made into an antidote that has saved the lives of many people bitten by taipans.

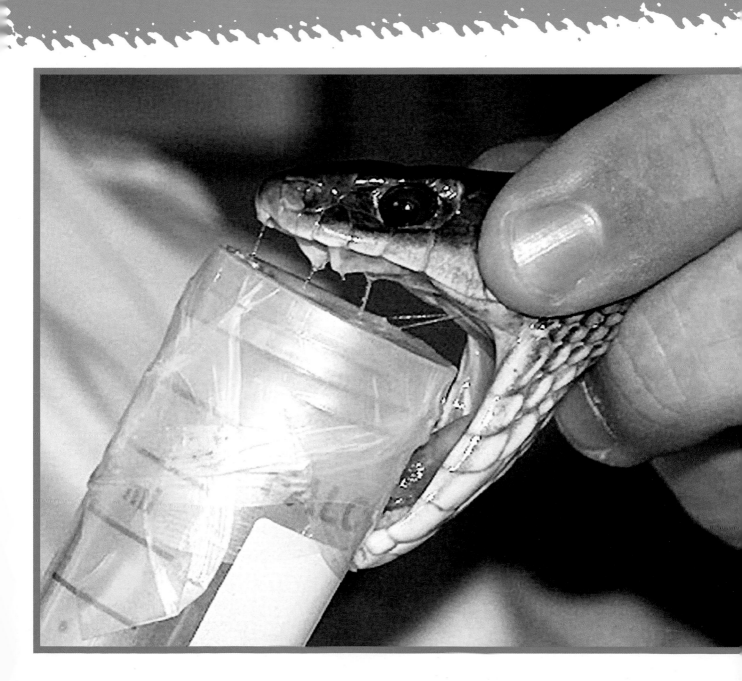

Super-quick mambas

Black mambas are found in many parts of Africa, mainly south of the Sahara Desert. These slithering reptiles are the fastest land snakes. They are also very bad-tempered, so you would not want to come face-to-face with one.

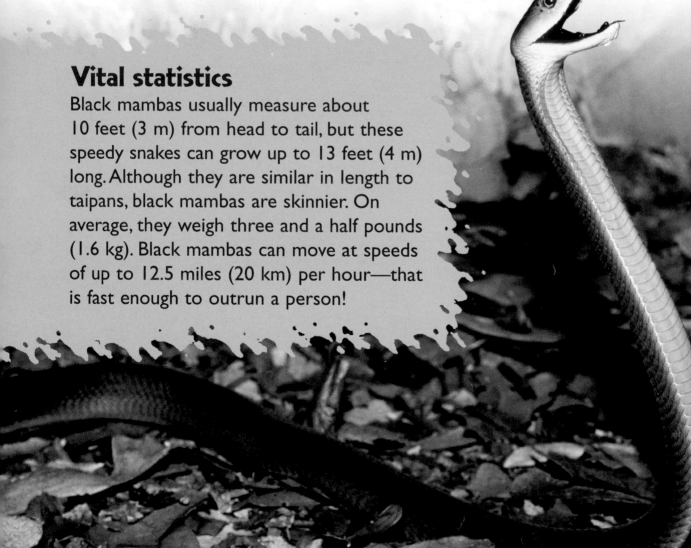

Vital statistics

Black mambas usually measure about 10 feet (3 m) from head to tail, but these speedy snakes can grow up to 13 feet (4 m) long. Although they are similar in length to taipans, black mambas are skinnier. On average, they weigh three and a half pounds (1.6 kg). Black mambas can move at speeds of up to 12.5 miles (20 km) per hour—that is fast enough to outrun a person!

Encounters with people

Like most venomous snakes, black mambas would rather avoid humans. But if they feel threatened, these deadly snakes will attack and use their speed to make a quick escape.

The bite of the black mamba is deadly, and it will kill a human within about four hours. Before the antidote for black mamba venom was made, no one bitten by a black mamba ever survived the attack.

How they kill

Black mambas have very good eyesight, which helps them find their victims. They usually prey on birds and rodents such as rats. When they attack, they rear up, lifting their head about three feet (0.9 m) off the ground. The snakes inject venom into their prey through the hollow fangs at the front of their mouth.

This deadly poison suffocates the prey, and the mamba eats it immediately. Although black mambas are skinny snakes, they can fit food up to four times the size of their head into their mouth! Black mambas can even dislocate their lower jaw to make room for large prey.

More about mambas

Baby black mambas

Female black mambas make nests out of rotting leaves, where they lay up to 15 eggs. As the leaves rot, they give off heat that helps to hatch the young.

As soon as they are born, the snakes can catch small prey such as mice. They grow very quickly, and are six and a half feet (2 m) long at a year old.

In a black mamba's mouth

Black mambas are not really black as their name suggests. In fact, they are a dark olive to brown color. They are called "black" because the inside of their mouth is black.

When a black mamba feels threatened, it opens its mouth wide enough to show off the dark color and scare off the predator.

Real-life story

In May 2004, snake collector Garrick Wales died from a snake bite. A box containing four snakes, including a deadly black mamba, was found on the road near his body. Garrick had ordered the snakes from a reptile dealer in Florida and had just collected them. Luckily, the boy who found the box of snakes did not open it!

Fact!

A black mamba has enough venom in its fangs to kill 10 adults.

Killer king cobras

King cobras are found in India and southeast Asia. Their unusual, hooded head makes king cobras easy to recognize.

King cobras are the snakes seen in some films in which a snake charmer plays music to lure the giant snake out of its basket.

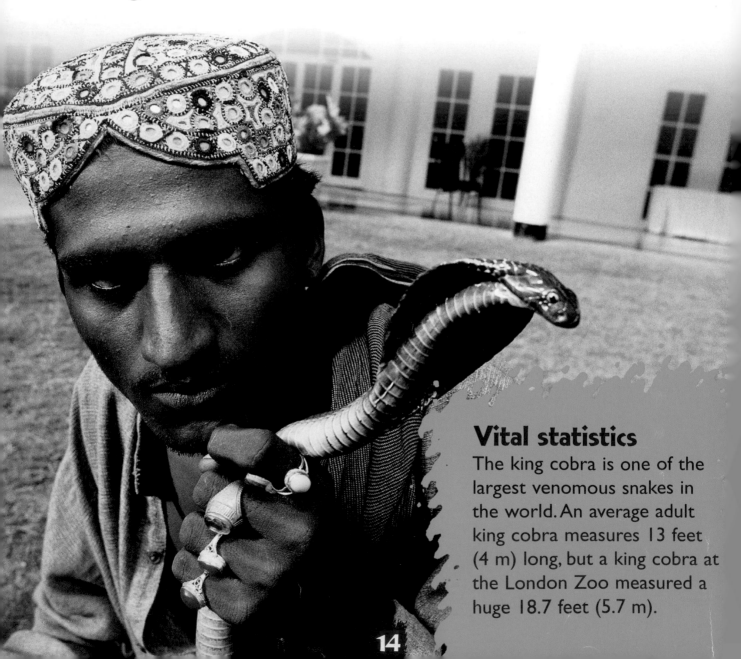

Vital statistics

The king cobra is one of the largest venomous snakes in the world. An average adult king cobra measures 13 feet (4 m) long, but a king cobra at the London Zoo measured a huge 18.7 feet (5.7 m).

King cobra young

King cobras lay between 20 and 50 eggs, which hatch after 60 to 70 days. Unlike many other snakes, male and female king cobras stay together to protect their nest.

Encounters with people

King cobras attack people only in self-defense or to protect their eggs. However, each year these deadly snakes kill about five people. A single bite can kill a person in 15 minutes.

Fact!

A king cobra has fake eyespots on the back of its hood to scare away other animals.

How they kill

These dangerous creatures are unusual because they prey on other snakes. Like some reptiles, such as Komodo dragons, they hunt by flicking their tongue in and out of their mouth.

This is how they smell their prey. King cobras sink their fangs into the unsuspecting victim, killing it quickly. After a meal, the snakes do not need to eat again for at least a few weeks.

Poisonous sea kraits

Sea kraits live in the shallow, tropical reefs of Bangladesh, Myanmar, Thailand, Malaysia, and Singapore.

Although they live mainly in the water, sea kraits return to land to shed their skin, to mate, and to lay eggs.

Vital statistics

Compared to many snakes, sea kraits are small. They usually grow to about four feet (1.2 m) long. Sea kraits have a flat tail that acts like a rudder to help them swim quickly. They also have special flaps over their nostrils to keep out water.

Encounters with people

Luckily for divers, these sea-living snakes are not very aggressive. Like most snakes, they would much rather avoid humans.

However, fishermen are sometimes bitten when they accidentally tangle the snakes in their nets. The sea kraits attack as the fishermen sort their catch.

Survival

Some sea kraits have been trapped and killed for their skin, which is used to make leather. So many sea kraits have been killed that they have become extinct on some Japanese and Filipino islands.

To protect the kraits on the Fijian Islands, scientists have tried to transfer the snakes from one island to another. Unfortunately, the snakes keep swimming the three miles (5 km) to their original home!

How they kill

Sea kraits are highly poisonous. They have enough venom in their fangs to kill an adult with one bite. Fortunately, they prey mainly on eels and small fish. As they bite into their prey, they inject venom that kills their victim.

Giant bushmasters

Bushmasters are the largest of the poisonous snakes found in the Americas. They live in the moist tropical forests and mountainous regions of Nicaragua, Panama, Costa Rica, Trinidad, and Brazil.

Vital statistics

An average bushmaster grows to about 7 feet (2.1 m) long, but some have been recorded at 12 feet (3.7 m). These giant snakes have broad, wedge-shaped heads and bony points, similar to spurs, on their tails.

How they kill

Bushmasters are pit vipers. Pit vipers have two heat-sensitive pits, one on each side of their head between the eye and the nostril. These pits allow the snakes to sense the small mammals that they eat.

Bushmasters have hinged fangs that lie flat on the roof of their mouth. The fangs can be very long, reaching one and a half inches (35 mm) in a large snake. When the snake senses its prey, the sharp fangs move forward and poke out—just like a movie vampire's!

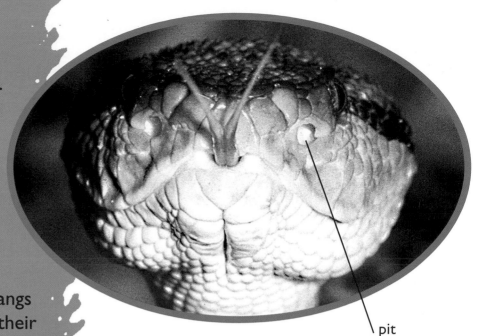

pit

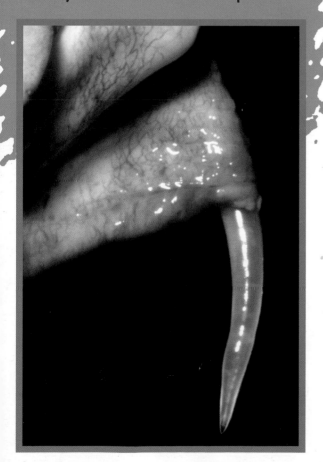

Baby bushmasters

When the female bushmaster is ready to lay eggs, she finds the burrow of a small animal. Sometimes she even shares the burrow with the animal that built it. After laying up to 12 eggs in the burrow, the snake wraps her body around the eggs until they hatch 76 to 79 days later.

Encounters with people

Bushmasters' venom is weak, but they produce a huge amount of it. A typical bushmaster bite injects .015 ounces (411 mg) of venom, compared to just .0005 ounces (15 mg) from a sea krait. Luckily, bushmasters are shy, and there are very few recorded deaths from their bites.

Ravenous rattlesnakes

There are 16 different types of rattlesnakes. Most of them live in the southwestern United States in very hot and dry habitats.

Vital statistics

Rattlesnakes can measure between three and five feet (0.9–1.5 m) in length. All rattlesnakes have a jointed "rattle" at the end of their tail that gives them their name.

How they kill

Rattlesnakes eat lizards and small rodents such as ground squirrels, rats, and mice. They inject their prey with venom.

If a larger animal is bitten by a rattlesnake and runs some distance before it dies, the snake will follow it and swallow it whole.

Encounters with people

Rattlesnakes try to warn off predators—including humans—by rattling their tail, which makes a noise like a shaker.

Although rattlesnake bites can be deadly, very few are fatal. Fatal cases occur when there are several bites, or when the victim is very old, very young, or already ill.

Survival

Rattlesnakes are greatly feared. For many years, "rattlesnake roundups" were held, with money paid for each skin from a dead rattlesnake.

It is because of events such as roundups that the number of rattlesnakes has fallen so dramatically. To prevent the snakes from becoming endangered, people are now being taught to respect and avoid them.

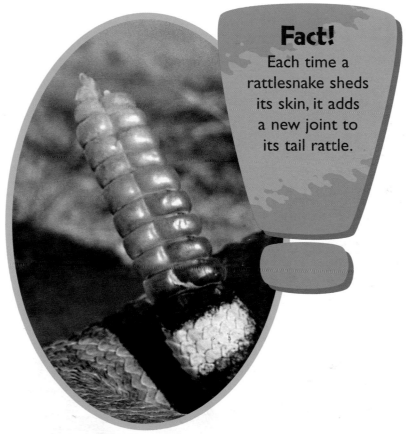

Fact!
Each time a rattlesnake sheds its skin, it adds a new joint to its tail rattle.

Deadly boomslangs

Boomslangs are found in Africa. They are often seen dangling from the branches of trees, where they hunt their prey— and scare innocent people looking for some shade!

Vital statistics

These greenish brown snakes grow to an average length of five feet (1.5 m), but boomslangs of up to six and a half feet (2 m) long have also been recorded.

Baby boomslangs

Female boomslangs lay between 8 and 23 eggs in hollow trees or in piles of leaves. The eggs hatch 70 to 100 days later, and the young snakes measure 11.5 to 15 inches (29–38 cm) long.

How they kill

These killer snakes eat chameleons, lizards, birds, frogs, and eggs. Many of their victims mistake the boomslangs for branches and even rest on them. When a boomslang sees prey, it moves its head from side to side and then pounces suddenly, moving its fangs as though it is chewing—but it is actually injecting lethal venom.

Encounters with people

Boomslang bites to humans are quite rare because the snakes are shy. If they come into contact with people, boomslangs usually try to move away. However, in 1957, snake expert Karl P. Schmidt died from a boomslang bite. He called in to work sick—and died from the bite just two hours later.

Scary spitting cobras

Just like king cobras, spitting cobras have hoods that they can puff out when they are angry. However, these snakes are also able to spray predators with venom.

There are several different kinds of spitting cobras, and most of them are found throughout Africa and Asia. They live in grassy, wooded areas and mangroves.

Vital statistics

Spitting cobras vary between four and six and a half feet (1.2–2 m) in length, depending on their species. Black-necked spitting cobras are the largest and can measure up to seven and a quarter feet (2.2 m). The western barred spitting cobra is the smallest—it measures only three to four feet (0.9–1.2 m).

Baby spitting cobras

These spitting snakes lay between 6 and 20 eggs in an abandoned animal burrow or a termite mound. When they hatch, the baby snakes are about eight inches (20 cm) long. Although the young snakes are small, they are just as venomous as the adult snakes.

Encounters with people

Sometimes spitting cobras slither into gardens and houses when they are looking for food, such as the rats and mice that feed on scraps left behind by humans. If a person is attacked by a spitting cobra, the bite can be fatal within six hours.

Fact!
Spitting cobras can shoot venom into the eyes of enemies eight feet (2.5 m) away.

Spitting venom

When spitting cobras feel threatened, they spray venom at their attacker to scare it away. The snakes push venom from the bottom of their fangs and force air out of their lungs at the same time, blowing venom at their victim.

How they kill

These dangerous snakes hunt mainly at night. They eat frogs, birds, and small mammals such as rodents. They use their fangs to hang on to prey after biting it, chewing to inject large amounts of deadly venom.

Massive anacondas

Anacondas are found in South America. They live near water in rain forests, grasslands, and forests.

Anacondas are active at night. During the day, they bathe in shallow water or lie on a low branch, often over water.

Vital statistics

Anacondas are one of the longest and heaviest types of snakes in the world. These amazing beasts can measure up to 30 feet (9 m) long. Large anacondas can be up to a foot (.3 m) thick and can weigh 550 pounds (250 kg). Female anacondas are usually heavier than males.

Fact!
Anacondas are great swimmers. They can stay underwater for up to 10 minutes!

What's for dinner?

Prey size is not a problem for these giant snakes. Anacondas eat many animals, including tapirs, peccaries, sheep, and large rodents such as capybaras, as well as fish, birds, and reptiles such as turtles. They have even been known to prey on jaguars!

How they kill

Anacondas are not poisonous snakes. Instead, they squeeze their prey to death. These giant killers lurk in water, grabbing their victims and pulling them under the surface. The prey either drowns or is crushed by the snake and swallowed whole.

Baby anacondas

Anacondas do not lay eggs. Instead, the females give birth to between 20 and 40 live babies. At birth, the snakes are two feet (0.6 m) long. Within hours, the babies can swim and hunt.

Encounters with people

Anacondas are quite slow moving, so they rarely kill people. However, because anacondas are so huge and people do not know enough about them, the snakes are killed out of fear.

Long reticulated pythons

Reticulated pythons live in southeast Asia and on several islands in the Pacific Ocean, such as Borneo, Java, Sumatra, and the Philippines. They are found near water in tropical rain forests and woodlands.

Vital statistics

Reticulated pythons are the longest snakes in the world. When they are fully grown, reticulated pythons can measure a staggering 33 feet (10 m). However, they are not as heavy as anacondas—the heaviest reticulated python weighed 250 pounds (113 kg).

How they kill

Reticulated pythons eat small mammals, birds, and some reptiles. They ambush their prey, waiting in trees to drop down as the animal passes by. They hold their prey with their fangs and coil around it, squeezing the animal until it cannot breathe.

Real-life story

The Rainforest Reptile Refuge in British Columbia, Canada, reported that a reticulated python turned up in someone's bathroom. A woman heard noises, and when she investigated, she found a skinny—but very long—snake in her bathroom, searching for food.

The Refuge thought that the creature had probably been kept as a pet but that its owners abandoned it because it grew too big. The snake was starving and covered in mites. Fortunately, the woman was not sitting on the toilet when the snake made its entrance!

Baby pythons

A female reticulated python lays about 100 eggs. The mother wraps herself around the eggs and shudders. These shuddering movements help to keep the eggs warm until they hatch.

Fact!

Pythons can go a long time between meals— one at the London Zoo did not eat for 23 months.

Survival

The skin of reticulated pythons has a beautiful pattern. This, along with the large size of the snakes, means that they are hunted for their skin, which is made into leather goods such as boots. Although these snakes are not an endangered species, their numbers are falling. This is because each year hundreds of thousands of reticulated pythons are killed for their skins.

Key words

Abandoned
When something is left alone.

Aggressive
Bad-tempered and dangerous.

Antidote
The medicine given to combat the effect of snake venom—it is usually made from snakes' venom and is sometimes called anti-venom.

Brood
When female snakes keep eggs warm so that they hatch.

Burrow
A hole dug by an animal.

Capybara
A very large rodent.

Cold-blooded
An animal that has a body temperature that changes depending on how hot or cold its surroundings are.

Dislocate
To put something—such as a bone or a joint—out of its proper place.

Endangered species
A group of living things in danger of dying out completely.

Extinct
When a group of living things dies out completely.

Habitat
The place where particular plants and animals live.

Limbs
Arms or legs.

Mammal
An animal with fur or hair that feeds its young with its own milk. Most mammals give birth to live young.

Mangrove
A tropical swamp full of thick shrubs and trees.

Peccaries
Pig-like mammals that are found in South America.

Predator
An animal that hunts and eats other animals.

Prey
Animals hunted by other animals for food.

Reefs
Areas of coral in warm, shallow sea waters.

Reptiles
Cold-blooded animals that have backbones and scaly skin.

Rodents
The family of mammals that includes rats and mice.

Rudder
The part of a ship in the water that helps steer the boat.

Snake charmer
A person who plays a musical instrument to get a snake to "dance" to the music.

Species
A group of closely related animals that can breed with each other.

Tapirs
Pig-like mammals.

Venom
Poison. A snake with venom in its fangs is called venomous.

Web links

http://classroomclipart.com
Great photographs of all kinds of snakes.

http://www.rattlesnakes.com
Home page of the American International Rattlesnake Museum.

http://simonsnakesite.tripod.com
Lots of information and tips for new snake owners.

http://library.thinkquest.org/5409
Everything you ever wanted to know about snakes.

http://www.thematzats.com/snakes
Lots of interesting and fun snake-themed activities.

http://www.reptileallsorts.com/snake-legends.htm
Features myths and legends that include snakes.

Note to parents:
Every effort has been made to ensure that the Web sites in this book are suitable for children, that they are of the highest educational value, and that they contain no inappropriate or offensive material. However, due to the nature of the Internet, it is impossible to guarantee that the contents of these sites will not be altered. We strongly advise that Internet access be supervised by a responsible adult.

Index